DAILY HUNGER

Nina Nencheva

Contents

Silence

It is so quiet around

as if I have gone deaf.

I am leaning over

the window-sill,

dropped a bird's feather –

it jingled like a coin.

Wish

Forgiveness – like a slingshot

and silence is a stone.

The bow-string of wish

is being pulled back.

Your wish is not to hurt me,

but- to possess me dead.

Migraine flight

Steel rings round the head –

a spaceman's helmet

of thoughtlessness.

Hurt or tired – it's all the same –

you are already an astronaut

in the mother spaceship of Being.

Protection

The Moon is a round, huge pupil,

risen in the black iris of darkness.

I love you, earthly, fragrant night –

a benevolent Cyclops, who

silently laid paws on my head.

Night Sketches

Wet and muddy,

wind is rushing on the right

at unallowed, inadmissible speed.

Something took my breath away –

the traffic lights just crossed

the zebra, when the light was red.

Perfection

Two eyes, two ears,

altogether – stereo senses.

Subtle means of inquisition.

We are physically perfect –

like accurate precision tools

that measure sadness.

Boldness

The Moon's brightness

already blinds me.

I wear now moon glasses. As if

cosmos is on the verge of a disaster,

as the Moon challenges

the supremacy of the Sun.

After the Apocalypse

In the twilight chaos and whirl

of lights – scattered and crushed,

I step cautiously

and overcarefully.

All is to be first destroyed

to be set right finally.

Rain

The clouds' fountain poured

down streams like ropes.

And if I did not forebode that

He might turn off the tap,

I would rock for a while on

the swing, hung from the skies.

Fable

A solemnly venomous Mamba

tries to hypnotize me, but doesn't

suspect he's behind the glass wall

(it's his first day in the aquarium).

Ignorant and wild, how can he know

that I'm the milker of the snakes.

Motherhood

Galaxies recede

and people, likewise, retreat –

it's due to you, all-powerful alienation.

We search to find

into the features of a child

the double of the Lord.

Winter date

Bewildered and confused

I squeeze a glove, embrace –

 a coat and kiss – a scarf.

I touch with breathless

thrill the cool sheath

of a dagger.

Dawn

I looked up to the sky

and it saw me, as well.

Then suddenly blushed,

turned pink all over,

but endured my insolent,

staring gaze.

Is it the rain knocking

on the window or a stray bird

 is dashing onto the window-panes?

Oh, dearest mother's worries,

do come in.

I didn't guess this could be you.

I felt a panic fear

of pans…Well, it's all right. Yet,

thus bending over the cooker,

forsaken in the corner of kitchen,

I saw the world around

from a different angle.

Why do we persist to know?

Is grave the place where

wisdom learning goes?

Nothing is by chance on earth.

Perhaps our memory somehow

after death continues to live.

Far away is death yet –

there, beyond the horizon,

with naked eye cannot be seen.

And still – it's so close

through binoculars – the dread

of the gap in between.

There is no other being,

as desperate as the man,

lying on his back,

staring at the ceiling,

decorated with a fly,

as if – with a brooch.

Don't write me letters!

Dedicate me a summer

instead of an ode or a sonnet

and I'll always know for certain

that spoken love

surpasses the written.

My balcony – right

opposite to your window,

just within

a gunshot distance.

Do not pull the trigger at night,

do not open the window, please.

Irreversible, riverlike,

asymmetrical time and me –

in its wild, sky-brown current,

floating – a solitary female –

a blond straw

for someone careless.

I hold tight the truth as if

a glass – lest it fall and break.

But it's so many-sided and edged,

that I know by now – what I hold

are the gathered pieces

of a broken glass.

Quietly lying in the grass,

through hoofs' and couch clatter

I overhear: a father is reproaching

his child, "How bad, ill-bred you are!"

And a pear-blossom falls from

the cherry-tree above – into my lap.

You were kissing me

under the chestnut trees, wet with rain,

when the sky took a picture of us

with a lightning flash. Then developed

it and laid it on a cloud to dry –

a longing for the impossible, a dewy sigh.

I have not encountered by now

a more exquisite knitting stitch –

lace of a dandelion,

a fishing-net of cobweb, where falls

the spider's victim as a catch.

Alas, there's perfidy in finesse.

I was awakened by a strange

noise in a velvet silence:

 Drip-drop-drop… Ah, yes.

The wall clock's gently dripping.

Master workers will be needed

for the roof of time is leaking.

We broke the terrarium

at home. Already we live

in conformity with nature –

stinging artlessly, inevitably and

detesting each other naturally.

Yet, there's ecology in alienation.

Seaweeds – my favorite flowers,

but no one changes the water

in their vase… They come to life

in a moment – like Ida's flowers:

bedouins on a two-humped wave,

roaming the sea - Sahara.

The headlights of a puddle

illuminated me. Realized suddenly

my short-sightedness. Finally

I puzzled it out – no doubt

the Sun is a spy, who follows me

around wherever I go.

Poets – tender, fragile beings,

tense, because straining to keep

the worlds swaying

in your tender glass-vessel.

I do bless your delicacy, into which

overprecious liquid was poured.

What a negligence –

I have always been late

for our dates!

I came on time just once –

when we parted…

It's through a cream

lace curtain what I see:

the orange tone in the skies'

complexion, a kiwi slice of blue,

and in between - my messy life.

The Sun blew in,

the wind shone brightly.

God sighed in Swahili

quietly.

The comet is a dog

that wags its tail,

the dead are species,

living in the ground. Without

doubt the poet is an alien -

he has metaphors

for breakfast and on

early mornings walks

a salamander on a lead.

We are lying naked

on the bed sheets like

in a Muslim burial.

Just cherish the nakedness

of a love moment –

an innocent dead man

rolls down out of

the coffin of the sheets,

then rises and ascends.

I'm talking with the light –

an elderly passenger,

who started her journey

as a girl, and arrived –

a white-haired old woman.

But we don't know what

she looked like as a girl.

For that reason her age

doesn't impress us so.

When you smile, recalling

something funny or frown

with a sudden pain,

I yearn to smooth your wrinkles

out with a tender iron.

In what suitcase did you

carry that dear face of yours-

a little bit of gloomy,

half–grinning mackintosh?

Oh, that darkness –

her face is so close to mine

that I can't see a feature –

just the black eyes,

enlarged to infinity.

Living in an optical illusion,

due to lack of distance,

every night I fall asleep

in the arms of the unknown.

I saw you in the crowd -

bemused and thoughtful,

looking down at you feet,

and understood -

it was written: although

you are being perfect,

you can't evoke

a feeling, as you are

indifferent to me.

I was in such a hurry

for twenty years now

to grow up and mature.

However, when I rose to

the top, standing upright -

negligent and autonomous,

a child like a Sisyphus stone

just rolled me down

to the beginning.

As for feelings I am like

a blind man – able to see

with my hands. Knowing

a priori: sadness is liquid and

grief is dry, I'm touching

my face – vertical moisture

is running down. Oh, there is

still hope – I don't love you

but - your lack of concern.

Then he sold his past

with an estate agent

to strangers from a far province –

a crumbling patio house

with uncosy exposure.

But he still receives tax bills

and electricity charges.

Maybe he was not erased

from the Property register.

Returning home I found –

a window was broken

and there was a hole

in the curtain… Then

I worked it out: it was you.

When going past my house

you threw a glance –

as if airy, as if random –

at my room.

A microscopic speck of dust –

a particle, only visible in

the sun's spotlight,

is rushing to a disaster -

the black hole of my eye.

An ancient civilization

 just vanished in an instant.

I felt crushed – a Gulliver,

heart-broken by his own size.

The body of Time was

found, as said - at the corner

of world and fantasies,

two blocks after reality,

and actually –

between the pages

of a wise book.

Who has been wasting

his time to kill it again?

All that I don't have...

And day by day, my empty

chest is getting fuller.

Now I have memories,

encounters, fulfilled whims,

but I'm poorer than then.

It's not just daily bread,

my friend, it's daily hunger

that we need to have.

Poet

When he dies one day

they will bury his soul.

Eternal is flesh and genes have

gossiped his lips, cheekbones,

and profile to children.

Yet his deceased soul

would turn over in grave,

as there isn't a gene

for a genious feeling.

A high wall and bloody

feud divide the lovers.

What if the interference

of families wasn't dramatized

unnecessarily?

Wasn't that the magnifying

glass that overstated

a hundred times a love,

prone to exaggeration.

Life is simmering slowly

on the round hot plate

of monotonous daily routine,

turned on by a fairy

who is world-unknown.

However, it isn't about her,

it's about what is at the top

 of the simmering pot – oh, god,

is it scum or is it cream?

A revelation– a cyclone out

of the blue knocked him down

and scattered his thoughts

in thousand bits.

He has knelt down in the

concentric circles of debris –

lines of magnetic fields.

Afterwards he reads

the dictionary like a novel.

At the Chemist

From dawn to dusk

the pharmacist fusses around,

searches the full shelves,

then he enters the back room,

checking the list of ointments,

capsules and tablets.

He has been seeking a remedy for

sensitivity (or a cure for death).

Doesn't remember if they have.

The fish began crying

but no one saw his tears.

Others concluded rashly:

water is rising, due to

global warming.

The destiny of sadness—

what liberty of morals

and what devotion –

to be married to everybody.

Starting over always

on a clean slate

and despite being a path

that has a past, I start

each day from the beginning.

Although there is repetition,

at night, when going to sleep

I feel certain: a mayfly lacks

this joy to start over again.